"The Art of Negotiation: Home Buying Edition"

Table of Contents

Introduction:	1
Chapter 1: Understanding the Home Buying Market	4
Chapter 2: Preparing for Negotiation: Essential Tools and Mindset	6
Chapter 3: Setting Your Budget: Beyond the Mortgage	8
Chapter 4: Researching Neighborhoods and Property Values	10
Chapter 5: Making an Offer: Crafting a Winning Proposal	13
Chapter 6: Navigating the Home Inspection Process	15
Chapter 7: Securing Financing: From Pre-Approval to Closing	17
Chapter 8: Understanding Closing Costs and Finalizing the Deal	19
Chapter 9: Settling In: Post-Purchase Checklist and Moving Tips	21
Chapter 10: Home Maintenance and Upkeep: Keeping Your Investment in Top Shape	23
Chapter 11: Energy Efficiency and Sustainability: Reducing Costs and Environmental Impact	26
Chapter 12: Understanding Property Taxes and Insurance: Managing Costs and Coverage	28
Chapter 13: Home Renovations and Upgrades: Enhancing Value and Functionality	31
Chapter 14: Navigating the Real Estate Market: Buying and Selling Strategies	34
Chapter 15: Preparing for Moving Day: Tips and Best Practices	36

Introduction:

In today's competitive real estate market, buying a home is more than just finding a place to live—it's an artful negotiation dance that involves strategy, timing, and an understanding of both market dynamics and personal priorities. "The Art of Negotiation: Home Buying Edition" is crafted to be your comprehensive guide through this intricate process, offering insights and tactics that can transform you from a novice into a skilled negotiator.

The journey of home buying can often seem daunting, filled with jargon, emotional highs and lows, and a myriad of decisions. This book aims to demystify the process by breaking down each step, providing clear strategies, and equipping you with the knowledge needed to approach negotiations with confidence and acumen.

Understanding the Home Buying Market

"The Art of Negotiation: Home Buying Edition"

Before diving into the nuances of negotiation, it is crucial to understand the landscape you are entering. The home buying market is influenced by a variety of factors including economic conditions, interest rates, and local real estate trends. Grasping these elements will not only prepare you for negotiations but also help you make informed decisions that align with your long-term goals.

Preparing for Negotiation: Essential Tools and Mindset

Negotiation begins long before you make your first offer. Preparation is key. This section will guide you through setting clear objectives, understanding your financial limits, and preparing psychologically for the negotiation process. You'll learn about the importance of having a well-defined strategy and how to cultivate the mindset of a successful negotiator.

Setting Your Budget: Beyond the Mortgage

A common misconception is that your budget should only include the mortgage payment. In reality, there are numerous additional costs to consider, such as property taxes, insurance, and maintenance. This chapter will help you build a comprehensive budget that accounts for all these variables, ensuring that you're financially prepared for the home you wish to buy.

Researching Neighborhoods and Property Values

Knowing the area in which you're buying is as important as the property itself. This chapter will delve into effective methods for researching neighborhoods, understanding local market trends, and evaluating property values. Armed with this information, you'll be in a stronger position to negotiate and make a well-informed offer.

The Power of an Agent: Finding the Right Professional

A real estate agent can be a powerful ally in your home-buying journey. This chapter discusses how to find a reputable agent who understands your needs and can advocate on your behalf. You'll learn about the benefits of working with an experienced professional and how to select someone who will enhance your negotiating position.

Mastering the Offer: How to Present Your Best Bid

Crafting an offer involves more than just naming a price. This chapter covers the elements of a strong offer, including contingencies, earnest money, and terms that can sway a seller in your favor. Learn how to present an offer that stands out and increases your chances of success.

Negotiating Terms: More Than Just Price

Negotiation is not just about the price; it's about the terms and conditions of the sale. From closing dates to repair requests, this chapter explores various terms that can be negotiated and how to use them to your advantage.

"The Art of Negotiation: Home Buying Edition"

Handling Counteroffers: Strategies for Success

When your initial offer is met with a counteroffer, how you respond can make or break the deal. This chapter provides strategies for handling counteroffers effectively, ensuring that you stay in control and maintain a favorable position in negotiations.

The Home Inspection Process: What to Expect

A home inspection is a critical step in the buying process. This chapter will guide you through what to expect during the inspection, how to interpret the findings, and how to use them in negotiations to address any issues that may arise.

Navigating Appraisals and Lender Expectations

Understanding the appraisal process and lender requirements is crucial to closing the deal. This chapter covers how appraisals can affect your negotiations and what you need to know about meeting lender expectations.

Closing the Deal: Legalities and Final Steps

The closing process involves several legal and procedural steps. This chapter provides a detailed overview of what to expect during closing, including paperwork, final payments, and legal considerations.

Overcoming Common Pitfalls in Home Buying Negotiations

Even the most prepared buyers can encounter obstacles. This chapter addresses common pitfalls and how to overcome them, ensuring that you can navigate challenges effectively and keep your negotiations on track.

Leveraging Market Trends to Your Advantage

Market trends can provide valuable insights into when and how to negotiate. This chapter explores how to leverage current trends to strengthen your negotiating position and achieve a better deal.

Post-Purchase Considerations: Moving In and Making It Your Own

Once the deal is closed, the real work begins. This chapter discusses important considerations for moving in, settling into your new home, and making it truly your own.

Long-Term Strategies for Real Estate Investment

Buying a home is often the first step in a broader real estate investment strategy. This chapter outlines long-term strategies for maximizing the value of your property and preparing for future investments.

"The Art of Negotiation: Home Buying Edition"

Chapter 1: Understanding the Home Buying Market

Introduction to the Real Estate Market

The real estate market is a dynamic and multifaceted ecosystem influenced by various factors including economic conditions, interest rates, and local market trends. Understanding this market is crucial for making informed decisions and successfully negotiating the purchase of a home. This chapter delves into the essential elements of the home buying market, providing you with the foundational knowledge needed to navigate the complexities of real estate transactions.

Economic Factors and Their Impact

The broader economy has a significant impact on the real estate market. Economic indicators such as GDP growth, unemployment rates, and inflation affect housing demand and property values. For instance, during periods of economic growth, job creation and higher incomes can lead to increased demand for housing, driving up property prices. Conversely, during economic downturns, housing demand may decrease, leading to lower property values.

Interest rates also play a critical role in the housing market. Lower interest rates make borrowing more affordable, which can boost housing demand as more buyers enter the market. On the other hand, higher interest rates can reduce affordability, potentially cooling the market. Understanding current interest rates and their trends is essential for making strategic decisions about when to buy and how much you can afford.

Local Market Trends

Local real estate markets can vary significantly from national trends. Factors such as regional economic conditions, population growth, and housing supply and demand all influence local property values. Researching local market trends helps you gauge the current state of the market in the area where you're looking to buy. This includes analyzing recent sales data, understanding neighborhood dynamics, and identifying any emerging trends that could affect property values.

One effective way to research local market trends is to review recent home sales data in your desired neighborhood. This data provides insights into property values, the length of time homes stay on the market, and the types of properties that are in demand. Additionally, talking to local real estate agents can offer valuable perspectives on market conditions and trends specific to your target area.

Supply and Demand Dynamics

The balance between supply and demand is a fundamental driver of property values. When demand for homes exceeds the available supply, prices tend to rise. This scenario often occurs in competitive markets where there are more buyers than available properties. Conversely, when there is an oversupply of homes and demand is weak, prices may stagnate or decrease.

"The Art of Negotiation: Home Buying Edition"

Factors influencing supply and demand include population growth, housing construction rates, and changes in local employment patterns. For example, a growing job market can attract new residents, increasing demand for housing. Conversely, an oversupply of new construction without corresponding demand can lead to price reductions.

Seasonal Trends

Real estate markets also experience seasonal fluctuations. Typically, the market is more active during the spring and summer months when weather conditions are favorable and families prefer to move before the start of the school year. Conversely, the market tends to slow down during the fall and winter months as fewer buyers and sellers are active. Understanding these seasonal trends can help you time your purchase strategically and take advantage of opportunities when the market is less competitive.

The Role of Government Policies

Government policies and regulations can also impact the real estate market. For instance, changes in tax laws, mortgage regulations, and housing incentives can influence buyer behavior and market conditions. Keeping abreast of any relevant policy changes can help you anticipate their effects on the market and adjust your strategy accordingly.

Analyzing Market Reports and Data

To make well-informed decisions, it's essential to analyze various market reports and data sources. Reports from real estate agencies, government housing agencies, and market analysts provide valuable information on current market conditions, trends, and forecasts. By reviewing these reports, you can gain insights into market dynamics and make more informed decisions about your home purchase.

Utilizing Technology for Market Research

In the digital age, technology has revolutionized the way we conduct market research. Online tools and platforms offer access to a wealth of information, including property listings, market trends, and neighborhood statistics. Websites such as Zillow, Redfin, and Realtor.com provide comprehensive data on property values, sales history, and local market trends. Utilizing these tools can enhance your research efforts and provide a clearer picture of the market.

The Importance of Professional Advice

While self-research is invaluable, seeking professional advice can provide additional insights and guidance. Real estate agents, appraisers, and market analysts can offer expertise and perspective that may not be readily available through online research alone. Engaging with professionals ensures that you have a well-rounded understanding of the market and helps you make more informed decisions.

Conclusion

"The Art of Negotiation: Home Buying Edition"

Understanding the home buying market is a critical first step in the negotiation process. By analyzing economic factors, local market trends, supply and demand dynamics, seasonal fluctuations, government policies, and utilizing both technology and professional advice, you'll be better equipped to navigate the complexities of the real estate market. This foundational knowledge will not only aid in making informed decisions but also enhance your negotiating position as you move forward in the home buying journey.

Chapter 2: Preparing for Negotiation: Essential Tools and Mindset

Introduction to Negotiation Preparation

Effective negotiation is a blend of strategy, preparation, and psychological readiness. Before you enter negotiations for buying a home, it's essential to arm yourself with the right tools and adopt the appropriate mindset. This chapter delves into the preparation process, offering practical advice on how to set yourself up for success and approach negotiations with confidence.

Setting Clear Objectives

Before negotiating, you must define your objectives. What are your primary goals in purchasing a home? Are you looking for a particular type of property, a specific location, or certain amenities? Establishing clear objectives will help you stay focused during negotiations and avoid getting swayed by factors that don't align with your needs.

1. **Identify Your Must-Haves vs. Nice-to-Haves**: Distinguish between essential features that you must have and additional features that would be desirable but are not critical. This distinction helps you prioritize your needs and remain steadfast in negotiations.
2. **Determine Your Budget**: Understand your financial limits, including how much you can afford for a down payment, monthly mortgage payments, and other associated costs. This financial clarity will guide your negotiations and prevent you from overextending yourself.

Understanding Your Financial Position

Your financial position plays a crucial role in negotiations. Before entering negotiations, ensure that you have a thorough understanding of your financial situation.

1. **Get Pre-Approved for a Mortgage**: A pre-approval letter from a lender demonstrates your seriousness and financial capability to sellers. It provides a clear picture of how much you can borrow and reassures sellers of your ability to complete the purchase.
2. **Review Your Credit Report**: Your credit score can significantly impact the mortgage terms you receive. Check your credit report for any inaccuracies and address any issues that could affect your ability to secure favorable financing.
3. **Calculate Total Costs**: Beyond the mortgage, account for additional expenses such as property taxes, insurance, and maintenance. Understanding these costs ensures that you are financially prepared for the home you wish to buy.

"The Art of Negotiation: Home Buying Edition"

Research and Knowledge Gathering

Knowledge is power in negotiations. The more you know about the property, the market, and the seller, the better equipped you will be.

1. **Research the Property**: Gather information on the property's history, including past sales, renovations, and any issues or disputes. This background knowledge can provide leverage during negotiations.
2. **Analyze Comparable Sales**: Look at recent sales of similar properties in the area to gauge a fair price. This information helps you make a competitive offer and supports your negotiating position.
3. **Understand Seller Motivations**: Try to learn why the seller is moving and how quickly they need to sell. This insight can help you tailor your negotiation strategy to address their motivations and increase your chances of success.

Developing a Negotiation Strategy

A well-thought-out strategy can make a significant difference in negotiations. Develop a plan that outlines how you will approach various aspects of the negotiation.

1. **Establish Your Opening Offer**: Decide on an initial offer based on your research and budget. Ensure that your opening offer is reasonable but leaves room for negotiation.
2. **Plan for Counteroffers**: Anticipate possible counteroffers from the seller and prepare responses for different scenarios. Knowing how to handle counteroffers allows you to remain flexible and adaptable during negotiations.
3. **Set Negotiation Goals**: Determine what you hope to achieve through negotiation, such as a lower price, repairs, or specific terms. Having clear goals helps you stay focused and measure your success.

Cultivating the Right Mindset

Your mindset plays a crucial role in negotiations. Adopting a positive and resilient attitude can influence the outcome of your negotiations.

1. **Stay Confident**: Confidence is key to successful negotiations. Believe in the value you bring to the table and maintain a professional demeanor throughout the process.
2. **Be Patient**: Negotiations can be lengthy and complex. Patience allows you to make thoughtful decisions and avoid rushing into agreements that may not be in your best interest.
3. **Maintain Flexibility**: While it's important to have clear objectives, be open to adjusting your approach based on new information or changing circumstances. Flexibility helps you navigate negotiations effectively and find mutually beneficial solutions.

Utilizing Negotiation Tools

"The Art of Negotiation: Home Buying Edition"

Several tools and resources can assist you in preparing for negotiations and ensuring that you are well-equipped to handle the process.

1. **Negotiation Checklists**: Use checklists to ensure that you've covered all necessary aspects of the negotiation, from financial considerations to contract terms.
2. **Real Estate Agents**: A knowledgeable real estate agent can provide valuable insights and assistance throughout the negotiation process. They can help you navigate complex negotiations and advocate on your behalf.
3. **Negotiation Software and Apps**: Technology offers various tools for managing and tracking negotiations. Consider using apps and software to organize your strategy, track communications, and manage documents.

Conclusion

Preparing for negotiation is a critical step in the home buying process. By setting clear objectives, understanding your financial position, conducting thorough research, developing a strategic approach, cultivating the right mindset, and utilizing effective tools, you will be well-prepared to enter negotiations with confidence and achieve favorable outcomes. This preparation will not only enhance your negotiating skills but also contribute to a successful and satisfying home buying experience.

Chapter 3: Setting Your Budget: Beyond the Mortgage

Introduction to Budgeting for Home Buying

Setting a budget for buying a home involves more than just determining how much you can afford to borrow. It's a comprehensive process that includes understanding all the costs associated with purchasing a property and ensuring that your financial plan aligns with your long-term goals. This chapter explores the various elements of budgeting for a home purchase, helping you create a realistic and manageable financial plan.

Understanding Mortgage Affordability

Your mortgage is a significant component of your overall home-buying budget, but it's not the only factor. Before diving into your budget, it's crucial to understand the affordability of your mortgage based on your income, expenses, and financial goals.

1. **Calculate Your Monthly Mortgage Payment**: Use a mortgage calculator to estimate your monthly payments based on different loan amounts, interest rates, and loan terms. This will give you an idea of how much you can afford to pay each month.
2. **Consider Debt-to-Income Ratio**: Lenders often use your debt-to-income (DTI) ratio to determine how much you can borrow. Your DTI ratio compares your total monthly debt payments to your gross monthly income. A lower DTI ratio indicates better financial health and may qualify you for more favorable loan terms.

"The Art of Negotiation: Home Buying Edition"

3. **Evaluate Interest Rates and Loan Terms**: The interest rate and loan term (e.g., 15 years vs. 30 years) affect your monthly payments and the total cost of the loan. Compare different loan options to find the best combination that fits your budget.

Beyond the Mortgage: Additional Costs

In addition to the mortgage, there are several other costs to consider when setting your home-buying budget.

1. **Down Payment**: The down payment is a percentage of the home's purchase price paid upfront. The amount required varies based on the type of mortgage and your financial situation. Conventional loans often require a 20% down payment, while other loan types, such as FHA loans, may require less.
2. **Closing Costs**: Closing costs include fees for services and paperwork required to finalize the home purchase. These can include loan origination fees, appraisal fees, title insurance, and escrow fees. Closing costs typically range from 2% to 5% of the purchase price.
3. **Property Taxes**: Property taxes are recurring expenses based on the assessed value of your home. These taxes vary by location and can impact your monthly budget. Research local property tax rates to estimate this expense.
4. **Homeowners Insurance**: Homeowners insurance protects your property and belongings against damage or loss. The cost of insurance can vary based on factors such as location, coverage level, and property value.
5. **Home Maintenance and Repairs**: Owning a home comes with ongoing maintenance and repair responsibilities. Budget for routine maintenance tasks (e.g., lawn care, HVAC servicing) and unexpected repairs (e.g., plumbing issues, roof leaks).
6. **Utilities and HOA Fees**: Utilities such as water, electricity, and gas are additional monthly expenses. If your property is part of a homeowners association (HOA), you may also have HOA fees that cover communal maintenance and amenities.

Building a Comprehensive Budget

To effectively manage your finances, build a comprehensive budget that includes all the costs associated with homeownership.

1. **Create a Detailed Budget Plan**: List all expected expenses related to buying and owning a home. Include your mortgage payment, down payment, closing costs, property taxes, insurance, maintenance, and other recurring costs.
2. **Set Aside an Emergency Fund**: An emergency fund is crucial for unexpected expenses or financial setbacks. Aim to save at least three to six months' worth of living expenses in an accessible account.
3. **Track Your Spending**: Regularly monitor your spending to ensure that you stay within your budget. Use budgeting tools or apps to help track expenses and adjust your budget as needed.

4. **Review and Adjust Your Budget Regularly**: Your financial situation may change over time, so review and adjust your budget periodically. This ensures that your budget remains aligned with your financial goals and any changes in your income or expenses.

Long-Term Financial Planning

Purchasing a home is a long-term financial commitment, and it's important to consider how it fits into your overall financial plan.

1. **Assess Your Financial Goals**: Consider how buying a home aligns with your long-term financial goals, such as saving for retirement or funding your children's education. Ensure that your home purchase doesn't compromise your ability to achieve these goals.
2. **Plan for Future Expenses**: Anticipate future expenses related to homeownership, such as major repairs or renovations. Budget for these expenses in advance to avoid financial strain.
3. **Evaluate the Impact on Your Financial Future**: Consider how the home purchase will affect your financial future, including your ability to save, invest, and manage debt. Ensure that the purchase supports your overall financial well-being.

Conclusion

Setting a budget for buying a home involves careful consideration of all associated costs beyond the mortgage. By calculating your monthly mortgage payment, accounting for down payments, closing costs, property taxes, insurance, and ongoing maintenance, you can create a comprehensive and realistic budget. Building an emergency fund, tracking your spending, and reviewing your budget regularly will help you manage your finances effectively and ensure that your home purchase aligns with your long-term financial goals. With a well-structured budget, you'll be better equipped to navigate the home-buying process and achieve a successful and satisfying purchase.

Chapter 4: Researching Neighborhoods and Property Values

Introduction to Neighborhood Research

When buying a home, selecting the right neighborhood is just as important as finding the perfect property. A neighborhood's characteristics can significantly impact your quality of life, property value, and long-term satisfaction. This chapter explores how to research neighborhoods and property values effectively, helping you make an informed decision about where to buy.

Evaluating Neighborhoods

1. **Assessing Safety and Crime Rates**: Safety is a top priority for many homebuyers. Research local crime rates through online crime maps, police reports, and community forums. Speak with current residents and local law enforcement to gain insights into the neighborhood's safety.

"The Art of Negotiation: Home Buying Edition"

2. **Exploring Local Amenities**: Consider the availability of amenities that are important to you, such as schools, parks, shopping centers, and medical facilities. Proximity to these amenities can enhance your daily convenience and overall satisfaction with the neighborhood.
3. **Evaluating Schools and Education**: If you have children or plan to in the future, research local schools and their ratings. Great schools can improve your quality of life and positively impact your property's value. Check school district websites, parent reviews, and academic performance data.
4. **Investigating Commute and Transportation**: Consider your daily commute and access to public transportation. A convenient commute can reduce stress and save time. Look into local transit options, road conditions, and proximity to major highways.
5. **Understanding the Community and Demographics**: Research the community's demographics and cultural aspects to ensure it aligns with your lifestyle and preferences. Attend local events, visit community centers, and engage with residents to get a feel for the neighborhood's character.
6. **Assessing Future Development**: Investigate any planned developments or zoning changes in the area. Future construction or changes in land use can affect property values and your living experience. Check with local government offices or planning departments for information on upcoming projects.

Researching Property Values

1. **Analyzing Comparable Sales (Comps)**: Compare the property you're interested in with similar properties that have recently sold in the area. This comparison, known as analyzing "comps," helps you understand the market value and determine if the property is priced appropriately.
2. **Studying Historical Price Trends**: Review historical price trends for the neighborhood to gauge how property values have changed over time. Look for patterns such as consistent growth or volatility, which can provide insights into the market's stability.
3. **Evaluating Property Features and Condition**: Assess the features and condition of the property relative to others in the area. Consider factors such as size, age, condition, and upgrades. Properties with superior features or in better condition may command higher prices.
4. **Reviewing Market Conditions**: Understand current market conditions, including supply and demand, interest rates, and economic factors. A hot market with high demand may drive up prices, while a buyer's market with excess inventory may offer more negotiating opportunities.

Utilizing Online Tools and Resources

1. **Real Estate Websites**: Online platforms such as Zillow, Redfin, and Realtor.com offer comprehensive data on property values, sales history, and neighborhood information. Use these resources to gather data and compare properties.
2. **Local Government Websites**: Check local government websites for property tax assessments, zoning regulations, and development plans. These sites often provide valuable information on the area's future and current conditions.

3. **Neighborhood Reviews and Forums**: Explore neighborhood reviews and forums for firsthand accounts from current residents. Websites like Nextdoor and local Facebook groups can provide insights into the community's atmosphere and any issues or benefits.

Engaging with Real Estate Professionals

1. **Working with a Real Estate Agent**: A knowledgeable real estate agent can provide valuable insights into neighborhoods and property values. They have access to detailed market data and can offer guidance based on their experience and local knowledge.
2. **Consulting a Real Estate Appraiser**: For a more detailed valuation of a specific property, consider hiring a real estate appraiser. An appraiser provides an independent assessment of the property's value based on various factors, including recent sales and property condition.
3. **Networking with Local Experts**: Engage with local experts such as property managers, builders, and neighborhood associations. They can offer additional perspectives and information about the area that may not be readily available through online research.

Making an Informed Decision

1. **Visit the Neighborhood**: Spend time in the neighborhood at different times of day to get a sense of traffic, noise levels, and general ambiance. Attend open houses and local events to interact with residents and experience the community firsthand.
2. **Compare Your Options**: Weigh the pros and cons of different neighborhoods and properties based on your research. Consider factors such as safety, amenities, property values, and your personal preferences.
3. **Trust Your Instincts**: While research and data are essential, trust your instincts when evaluating neighborhoods and properties. If a neighborhood feels right and meets your needs, it may be the ideal place for your new home.

Conclusion

Researching neighborhoods and property values is a critical step in the home-buying process. By evaluating safety, amenities, schools, transportation, and future development, you can choose a neighborhood that aligns with your lifestyle and long-term goals. Analyzing property values through comparable sales, historical trends, and market conditions ensures that you make a well-informed decision about your investment. Utilizing online tools, engaging with real estate professionals, and visiting neighborhoods firsthand will further enhance your research and help you find the perfect home in the right location.

Chapter 5: Making an Offer: Crafting a Winning Proposal

Introduction to Making an Offer

Once you've identified the right property and completed your research, the next step in the home-buying process is to make an offer. Crafting a compelling offer requires careful

"The Art of Negotiation: Home Buying Edition"

consideration of various factors to ensure that it is attractive to the seller while aligning with your own goals. This chapter explores the components of a strong offer, strategies for making a successful proposal, and the negotiation process.

Components of a Strong Offer

1. **Offer Price**: The offer price is a key element of your proposal. Base your offer on comparable sales, the property's condition, and current market conditions. While it's tempting to offer less to get a bargain, make sure your offer is realistic to avoid losing out on the property.
2. **Earnest Money Deposit**: An earnest money deposit demonstrates your commitment to the purchase. This deposit is typically 1% to 3% of the purchase price and is held in escrow until the sale is completed. A larger deposit can make your offer more attractive to sellers.
3. **Contingencies**: Contingencies are conditions that must be met for the sale to proceed. Common contingencies include a home inspection, appraisal, and financing. Clearly outline these conditions in your offer to protect yourself and ensure that you can back out if issues arise.
4. **Closing Date**: The closing date is when the sale is finalized, and ownership is transferred. Consider the seller's preferred timeline and align your proposed closing date accordingly. A flexible closing date can make your offer more appealing to sellers.
5. **Personal Letter**: A personal letter to the seller can make your offer stand out. Share your story, explain why you love the home, and highlight your connection to the community. A heartfelt letter can create an emotional connection and influence the seller's decision.

Strategies for a Successful Offer

1. **Make a Competitive Offer**: In a competitive market, offering a price close to or above the asking price may be necessary to secure the property. Work with your real estate agent to determine a competitive offer based on recent sales and market conditions.
2. **Include a Pre-Approval Letter**: A pre-approval letter from your lender confirms your financial capability to purchase the home. Including this letter with your offer demonstrates your seriousness and strengthens your proposal.
3. **Be Flexible with Terms**: Being flexible with terms such as the closing date or contingencies can make your offer more attractive. Consider accommodating the seller's preferences to increase your chances of acceptance.
4. **Consider an Escalation Clause**: In highly competitive situations, an escalation clause allows you to automatically increase your offer if another bid comes in higher. This clause specifies the maximum amount you're willing to pay and can help you remain competitive without overbidding initially.
5. **Offer a Larger Earnest Money Deposit**: Increasing your earnest money deposit can demonstrate your commitment and make your offer more appealing. A larger deposit can give sellers confidence in your intention to follow through with the purchase.

The Negotiation Process

"The Art of Negotiation: Home Buying Edition"

1. **Responding to Counteroffers**: Sellers may respond to your offer with a counteroffer, which may involve changes to the price, contingencies, or terms. Be prepared to review and negotiate these terms to reach a mutually acceptable agreement.
2. **Communicate Clearly**: Effective communication with the seller or their agent is crucial during negotiations. Clearly articulate your terms, be responsive to counteroffers, and address any concerns promptly to facilitate a smooth negotiation process.
3. **Know When to Compromise**: Negotiations often involve compromise. Identify your priorities and be willing to adjust less critical terms to reach an agreement. Flexibility can help you secure the property while still achieving your key goals.
4. **Seek Professional Guidance**: Your real estate agent plays a critical role in the negotiation process. Leverage their expertise to navigate counteroffers, provide strategic advice, and advocate on your behalf.

Finalizing the Offer

1. **Review the Contract**: Carefully review the purchase agreement and any associated documents before finalizing your offer. Ensure that all terms and conditions are accurately represented and that there are no errors or omissions.
2. **Sign and Submit**: Once you've reviewed and agreed to the terms, sign the offer and submit it to the seller. Your agent will facilitate this process and ensure that all necessary paperwork is completed and submitted on time.
3. **Await Response**: After submitting your offer, await the seller's response. They may accept your offer, reject it, or propose further negotiations. Be prepared to respond promptly to keep the process moving forward.

Conclusion

Making an offer on a home involves crafting a compelling proposal that reflects both your needs and the seller's preferences. By including key components such as a competitive offer price, earnest money deposit, contingencies, and a personal letter, you can create an attractive proposal. Employing strategies like being flexible with terms, considering an escalation clause, and offering a larger earnest money deposit can enhance your chances of success. Throughout the negotiation process, effective communication, professional guidance, and a willingness to compromise will help you navigate offers and counteroffers. With a well-prepared and strategic approach, you'll be better positioned to secure your desired home.

Chapter 6: Navigating the Home Inspection Process

Introduction to Home Inspections

A home inspection is a crucial step in the home-buying process that helps you assess the condition of a property before finalizing the purchase. It provides valuable information about potential issues and repairs, ensuring that you make an informed decision. This chapter explores the home inspection process, including what to expect, how to interpret inspection reports, and how to address any issues that arise.

"The Art of Negotiation: Home Buying Edition"

Understanding the Home Inspection Process

1. **Choosing a Qualified Home Inspector**: Select a licensed and experienced home inspector to conduct the inspection. Ask for recommendations from your real estate agent, friends, or family, and check the inspector's credentials and reviews. A qualified inspector will provide a thorough and accurate assessment of the property.
2. **Scheduling the Inspection**: Coordinate with the seller to schedule the home inspection. Ideally, the inspection should take place shortly after your offer is accepted and before the closing date. This timing allows you to address any issues that may arise and renegotiate terms if necessary.
3. **Preparing for the Inspection**: Prepare for the inspection by providing the inspector with access to all areas of the home, including the attic, basement, and crawl spaces. Ensure that utilities are turned on, and remove any obstructions that may hinder the inspector's work.

What to Expect During the Inspection

1. **Inspection Overview**: The inspector will evaluate various components of the home, including the structure, roof, plumbing, electrical systems, HVAC systems, and appliances. They will check for signs of damage, wear, and potential issues that may require repair or maintenance.
2. **Inspection Duration**: A typical home inspection takes two to three hours, depending on the size and condition of the property. The inspector will examine both visible and accessible areas, as well as perform tests and checks as needed.
3. **Receiving the Inspection Report**: After the inspection, you will receive a detailed report outlining the inspector's findings. The report will include information on the property's condition, any defects or issues, and recommendations for repairs or maintenance.

Interpreting the Inspection Report

1. **Understanding Common Issues**: Familiarize yourself with common issues that may be identified during the inspection, such as roof damage, plumbing leaks, electrical problems, or foundation issues. Understanding these issues will help you assess their significance and potential impact on the property.
2. **Prioritizing Repairs**: Review the inspection report and prioritize repairs based on their severity and impact. Focus on major issues that could affect the safety, functionality, or value of the property. Minor cosmetic issues can often be addressed after purchase.
3. **Evaluating Repair Costs**: Obtain estimates for any required repairs or maintenance from qualified contractors. This will help you understand the potential costs involved and determine how they may affect your overall budget and decision-making.

Negotiating Repairs and Terms

1. **Requesting Repairs**: Based on the inspection report, you may request that the seller address specific issues before closing. Common requests include repairs to major systems, such as HVAC or plumbing, or addressing safety concerns.

"The Art of Negotiation: Home Buying Edition"

2. **Renegotiating the Purchase Price**: If significant issues are identified, you may choose to renegotiate the purchase price to account for the cost of repairs. Provide evidence from the inspection report and repair estimates to support your request.
3. **Considering Repair Credits**: Instead of requesting repairs, you may negotiate a repair credit, which is a financial concession from the seller to cover the cost of repairs. This allows you to address issues after purchase and provides flexibility in managing repairs.
4. **Deciding to Proceed or Withdraw**: Depending on the inspection findings and negotiations, you must decide whether to proceed with the purchase, renegotiate the terms, or withdraw your offer. Consider the overall condition of the property, the significance of any issues, and your willingness to address them.

Finalizing the Inspection Process

1. **Reviewing Repair Agreements**: If repairs or credits are agreed upon, ensure that these terms are documented in the purchase agreement. Confirm that the seller fulfills their commitments before closing.
2. **Conducting a Re-Inspection**: If significant repairs were made, consider scheduling a re-inspection to verify that the issues have been addressed properly. This step ensures that the repairs meet your expectations and are completed to your satisfaction.
3. **Preparing for Closing**: Once the inspection process is complete and any necessary agreements are in place, continue with the closing process. Ensure that all inspection-related conditions are met and that you're satisfied with the property's condition before finalizing the purchase.

Conclusion

Navigating the home inspection process is a vital part of buying a home. By selecting a qualified inspector, understanding what to expect, interpreting the inspection report, and negotiating repairs or terms, you can make informed decisions and ensure that your new home meets your standards. Addressing inspection issues proactively and incorporating them into your purchase agreement will help you avoid unexpected problems and enjoy peace of mind as you move forward with your home purchase.

Chapter 7: Securing Financing: From Pre-Approval to Closing

Introduction to Securing Financing

Securing financing is a critical step in the home-buying process that involves obtaining a mortgage to fund your purchase. This chapter provides a comprehensive guide to navigating the financing process, from getting pre-approved to closing on your loan. Understanding each step will help you secure the best financing terms and ensure a smooth transition to homeownership.

Getting Pre-Approved for a Mortgage

"The Art of Negotiation: Home Buying Edition"

1. **Understanding Pre-Approval vs. Pre-Qualification**: Pre-approval and pre-qualification are often confused, but they are distinct processes. Pre-qualification provides a general estimate of what you might be able to borrow based on your financial information. Pre-approval, on the other hand, involves a more detailed review of your financial situation and provides a formal commitment from the lender regarding the loan amount you qualify for.
2. **Gathering Documentation**: To get pre-approved, you will need to provide various documents to the lender, including:
    - Proof of income (e.g., pay stubs, tax returns)
    - Proof of assets (e.g., bank statements, retirement accounts)
    - Employment verification
    - Credit history and credit score
3. **Submitting Your Application**: Complete a mortgage application with your chosen lender. This will involve providing detailed financial information and authorizing the lender to perform a credit check. The lender will use this information to assess your ability to repay the loan and determine your pre-approved loan amount.
4. **Receiving Pre-Approval Letter**: Once the lender has reviewed your application and documentation, they will issue a pre-approval letter. This letter indicates the maximum loan amount you qualify for and serves as a valuable tool in making your offer more competitive.

Choosing the Right Mortgage

1. **Types of Mortgages**: Familiarize yourself with different types of mortgages to select the one that best fits your needs. Common types include:
    - **Fixed-Rate Mortgages**: Offer a stable interest rate and consistent monthly payments over the life of the loan.
    - **Adjustable-Rate Mortgages (ARMs)**: Feature an interest rate that changes periodically based on market conditions, potentially leading to fluctuating monthly payments.
    - **FHA Loans**: Backed by the Federal Housing Administration, these loans are often available to first-time buyers with lower credit scores and smaller down payments.
    - **VA Loans**: Offered to veterans and active-duty military personnel, these loans are backed by the Department of Veterans Affairs and often require no down payment.
2. **Comparing Interest Rates**: Shop around and compare interest rates from different lenders. Even a small difference in the interest rate can have a significant impact on your monthly payments and the total cost of the loan.
3. **Evaluating Loan Terms**: Consider the loan term, which is the length of time over which you will repay the loan. Common terms include 15 years and 30 years. Shorter terms typically have higher monthly payments but lower overall interest costs, while longer terms offer lower monthly payments but may result in higher total interest payments.

Applying for the Mortgage

"The Art of Negotiation: Home Buying Edition"

1. **Submitting the Loan Application**: After selecting a mortgage type and lender, submit a formal loan application. This will include detailed information about the property you're purchasing, your financial situation, and any other relevant details.
2. **Providing Additional Documentation**: Be prepared to provide additional documentation or information as requested by the lender. This may include updated financial statements, explanations for any discrepancies, or further proof of income or assets.
3. **Undergoing a Credit Check**: The lender will perform a credit check to assess your creditworthiness. A good credit score is essential for securing favorable loan terms. Address any credit issues or discrepancies before applying to improve your chances of approval.

The Loan Approval Process

1. **Loan Underwriting**: Once you've submitted your application, it will undergo underwriting, where the lender reviews all aspects of your financial situation and the property. The underwriter will assess the risk of lending and determine if your application meets the lender's criteria.
2. **Receiving the Loan Commitment**: If your application is approved, you will receive a loan commitment letter outlining the terms and conditions of your mortgage. Review this letter carefully to ensure that all terms align with what you discussed with your lender.
3. **Addressing Conditions**: The loan commitment may include conditions that must be met before final approval. Address any outstanding conditions promptly to avoid delays in the closing process.

Closing on the Loan

1. **Reviewing the Closing Disclosure**: Prior to closing, you will receive a Closing Disclosure, which details the final loan terms, including the interest rate, monthly payments, and closing costs. Review this document carefully to ensure that there are no discrepancies or unexpected charges.
2. **Preparing for Closing Costs**: Closing costs typically include fees for loan origination, appraisal, title insurance, and other services. Prepare to cover these costs, which are usually paid at the closing meeting.
3. **Attending the Closing Meeting**: The closing meeting is where you will finalize the purchase of your home. You will review and sign various documents, including the mortgage agreement and the deed. Ensure that you have all required documentation and funds available.
4. **Finalizing the Loan**: After signing the necessary documents and completing the closing process, your loan will be finalized, and the funds will be disbursed. You will receive the keys to your new home and officially become the owner.

Conclusion

Securing financing is a critical component of buying a home, involving steps from pre-approval to closing. By understanding the pre-approval process, choosing the right mortgage, applying for the loan, and navigating the approval and closing stages, you can secure favorable financing

"The Art of Negotiation: Home Buying Edition"

terms and ensure a smooth transition to homeownership. Working closely with your lender and addressing any requirements promptly will help you achieve your goal of owning a home with confidence and ease.

Chapter 8: Understanding Closing Costs and Finalizing the Deal

Introduction to Closing Costs

Closing costs are the fees and expenses associated with finalizing a real estate transaction. These costs can add up to a significant amount and are essential to understand as they directly impact the total amount of money you'll need to complete the purchase of your home. This chapter will guide you through the various types of closing costs, how to estimate and manage them, and what to expect during the final stages of the home-buying process.

Types of Closing Costs

1. **Loan-Related Costs**:
    - **Origination Fees**: These fees are charged by the lender for processing your loan application and preparing the necessary paperwork. They are typically a percentage of the loan amount.
    - **Points**: Points are upfront fees paid to reduce the interest rate on your mortgage. Each point typically costs 1% of the loan amount and can lower your monthly payments over the life of the loan.
    - **Appraisal Fee**: This fee covers the cost of the home appraisal, which assesses the property's value to ensure it meets the lender's requirements.
2. **Title and Legal Costs**:
    - **Title Search and Insurance**: A title search verifies that the property's title is clear of any liens or legal issues. Title insurance protects both the buyer and lender against any future claims on the property.
    - **Attorney Fees**: If you hire an attorney to assist with the closing process, their fees will be included in your closing costs. This is optional and depends on local regulations and personal preference.
3. **Property-Related Costs**:
    - **Home Inspection Fee**: If you had a home inspection done, this fee is typically paid at the time of the inspection, but it may be included in your closing costs if the seller agreed to reimburse you.
    - **Transfer Taxes**: Transfer taxes are imposed by local or state governments when the property title is transferred from the seller to the buyer. The amount varies by location.
4. **Prepaid Costs**:
    - **Prepaid Interest**: This covers the interest on your mortgage loan from the closing date to the end of the month. It ensures that your first mortgage payment is not due immediately.
    - **Property Taxes and Homeowners Insurance**: You may need to prepay a portion of property taxes and homeowners insurance into an escrow account to ensure that these expenses are covered when due.

"The Art of Negotiation: Home Buying Edition"

Estimating Closing Costs

1. **Using a Closing Cost Calculator**: Many online tools and calculators can help estimate closing costs based on your loan amount, property value, and location. These calculators provide a rough estimate and can help you budget accordingly.
2. **Reviewing the Loan Estimate**: Your lender is required to provide a Loan Estimate (LE) within three business days of receiving your application. This document outlines the estimated closing costs, loan terms, and other key details. Review it carefully to understand the costs you'll be responsible for.
3. **Comparing Estimates**: Obtain estimates from different lenders and compare them to ensure that you're getting the best deal. Differences in fees and charges can affect your overall closing costs and the affordability of your loan.

Managing and Paying Closing Costs

1. **Budgeting for Closing Costs**: Include closing costs in your home-buying budget to ensure that you have sufficient funds available. Consider setting aside additional savings to cover these expenses.
2. **Negotiating with the Seller**: In some cases, you may be able to negotiate with the seller to cover a portion of the closing costs. This is often done as part of the offer or during the negotiation process.
3. **Exploring Closing Cost Assistance Programs**: Some local or state programs offer assistance with closing costs for first-time homebuyers or low-to-moderate income buyers. Research available programs and check if you qualify for any financial assistance.

Finalizing the Deal

1. **Preparing for the Closing Meeting**: Before the closing meeting, review the Closing Disclosure, which details the final costs and terms of your loan. Ensure that all information is accurate and that there are no unexpected charges.
2. **Reviewing and Signing Documents**: At the closing meeting, you will review and sign various documents, including the mortgage agreement, deed, and closing disclosure. Take your time to read each document carefully and ask questions if needed.
3. **Transferring Funds**: Arrange for the transfer of funds to cover your closing costs. This is usually done via a certified or cashier's check, wire transfer, or other approved methods. Ensure that the funds are available and that you meet any deadlines set by the closing agent.
4. **Receiving the Keys**: Once all documents are signed and funds are transferred, you will receive the keys to your new home. At this point, the property is officially yours, and you can begin moving in and enjoying your new space.

Conclusion

Understanding and managing closing costs is an essential part of the home-buying process. By familiarizing yourself with the various types of costs, estimating them accurately, and preparing

"The Art of Negotiation: Home Buying Edition"

for the final steps of the transaction, you can ensure a smooth and successful closing experience. Effective budgeting, negotiation, and thorough review of all documents will help you navigate this critical stage and achieve your goal of homeownership with confidence.

Chapter 9: Settling In: Post-Purchase Checklist and Moving Tips

Introduction to Settling In

After closing on your new home, the excitement of becoming a homeowner is accompanied by the responsibilities of moving in and settling into your new space. This chapter provides a comprehensive checklist and practical tips to ensure a smooth transition from the purchase of your home to making it your own. From finalizing paperwork to organizing your move and acclimating to your new neighborhood, these steps will help you start this new chapter on the right foot.

Post-Purchase Checklist

1. **Change of Address**:
    - **Notify USPS**: Update your address with the United States Postal Service (USPS) to ensure that your mail is forwarded to your new home.
    - **Update Addresses**: Inform banks, credit card companies, insurance providers, and other important contacts of your new address. Don't forget to update your address with subscription services and online shopping accounts.
2. **Set Up Utilities**:
    - **Transfer or Set Up Utilities**: Arrange for the transfer or setup of essential utilities such as electricity, gas, water, internet, and cable. Contact utility providers to schedule installation or transfer dates.
    - **Confirm Service Activation**: Ensure that all utilities are activated and functioning properly before moving in. This includes checking that water, heat, and electricity are working.
3. **Home Security**:
    - **Change Locks**: For security reasons, consider changing the locks on your new home. This ensures that previous owners or anyone else with access to the old keys cannot enter your home.
    - **Install or Update Security Systems**: If your home has a security system, review and update it as necessary. Consider installing additional security measures if desired.
4. **Insurance**:
    - **Update Homeowners Insurance**: Confirm that your homeowners insurance policy is active and accurately reflects your new property. Review coverage to ensure it meets your needs and consider additional coverage if necessary.
5. **Document Organization**:
    - **File Important Documents**: Keep copies of important documents such as the purchase agreement, closing disclosure, mortgage agreement, and any warranties or manuals for appliances. Store these documents in a safe and accessible place.

"The Art of Negotiation: Home Buying Edition"

Moving Tips

1. **Create a Moving Plan**:
    - **Organize Your Move**: Develop a detailed moving plan that includes a timeline, packing strategy, and moving company arrangements. A well-organized plan helps reduce stress and ensures that all aspects of the move are covered.
    - **Hire Movers or Rent a Truck**: Decide whether to hire professional movers or rent a moving truck. Obtain quotes from moving companies and compare them to ensure you get the best value.
2. **Packing and Labeling**:
    - **Pack Strategically**: Pack your belongings in an organized manner, starting with non-essential items and leaving essentials for last. Use sturdy boxes and packing materials to protect your belongings during the move.
    - **Label Boxes**: Clearly label each box with its contents and the room it belongs to. This will make unpacking more efficient and help movers place boxes in the correct rooms.
3. **Preparing Your New Home**:
    - **Clean Before Moving In**: Consider cleaning your new home before moving in to ensure a fresh start. This may include vacuuming, dusting, and cleaning appliances and fixtures.
    - **Inspect and Address Issues**: Conduct a thorough inspection of your new home to identify any immediate issues or repairs needed. Address these concerns before unpacking to avoid disruptions.
4. **Settling In**:
    - **Unpack Systematically**: Unpack methodically, starting with essential items and moving to non-essentials. Organize each room as you unpack to create a functional and comfortable living space.
    - **Arrange Furniture and Decor**: Arrange furniture and decorate your home to suit your personal style. Take your time to create a layout that is both functional and aesthetically pleasing.
5. **Getting Acquainted with Your New Neighborhood**:
    - **Explore the Area**: Take some time to explore your new neighborhood. Visit local shops, restaurants, parks, and other amenities to familiarize yourself with the area.
    - **Meet Your Neighbors**: Introduce yourself to your new neighbors and build relationships within the community. Getting to know your neighbors can enhance your sense of belonging and provide valuable local insights.
6. **Establishing Routine**:
    - **Settle into a Routine**: Establish a daily routine that works for you and your family in your new home. This helps create a sense of normalcy and stability as you adjust to your new environment.

Conclusion

Settling into a new home involves more than just unpacking boxes; it's about making the space your own and integrating into a new community. By following a comprehensive post-purchase checklist, planning your move carefully, and taking the time to get acquainted with your new neighborhood, you can ensure a smooth transition and start enjoying your new home. With careful planning and organization, you'll be well on your way to making your new house a comfortable and welcoming home.

Chapter 10: Home Maintenance and Upkeep: Keeping Your Investment in Top Shape

Introduction to Home Maintenance

Maintaining your home is essential for preserving its value, ensuring its safety, and enhancing your quality of life. Regular maintenance and upkeep can prevent costly repairs and extend the lifespan of various components in your home. This chapter provides a comprehensive guide to home maintenance, covering essential tasks, seasonal upkeep, and tips for managing repairs effectively.

Essential Home Maintenance Tasks

1. **Routine Inspections**:
    - **Inspect the Roof**: Regularly check your roof for damaged shingles, leaks, or other issues. Addressing problems early can prevent more extensive damage and costly repairs.
    - **Check Gutters and Downspouts**: Clean gutters and downspouts to ensure proper drainage and prevent water damage to your home's foundation. Clogged gutters can lead to leaks and structural issues.
2. **HVAC System Maintenance**:
    - **Replace Air Filters**: Replace air filters in your heating, ventilation, and air conditioning (HVAC) system every 1-3 months to ensure optimal performance and air quality.
    - **Schedule Professional Servicing**: Have your HVAC system serviced by a professional annually to check for issues, clean components, and ensure efficient operation.
3. **Plumbing Maintenance**:
    - **Inspect Pipes**: Check for leaks, corrosion, or signs of wear in your pipes. Address any issues promptly to prevent water damage and costly repairs.
    - **Clean Drains**: Use drain cleaners or natural methods to prevent clogs in sinks, showers, and tubs. Regular cleaning can prevent backups and maintain proper drainage.
4. **Electrical System Checks**:
    - **Test Smoke and Carbon Monoxide Detectors**: Test and replace batteries in smoke and carbon monoxide detectors regularly. Ensure that these devices are functional and up to code.
    - **Inspect Electrical Outlets and Wiring**: Check for signs of wear or damage in electrical outlets and wiring. Address any issues immediately to prevent electrical hazards.

"The Art of Negotiation: Home Buying Edition"

Seasonal Home Maintenance

1. **Spring**:
   - **Clean Windows and Exterior**: Clean windows, siding, and outdoor surfaces to remove dirt and debris. This helps maintain curb appeal and prevents long-term damage.
   - **Inspect and Service HVAC System**: Prepare your HVAC system for the warmer months by having it serviced and ensuring that it's functioning efficiently.
2. **Summer**:
   - **Maintain Landscaping**: Keep your lawn, garden, and landscaping well-maintained. Trim shrubs, mow the lawn, and water plants as needed.
   - **Check for Pests**: Inspect your home for signs of pests, such as ants or termites. Address any infestations promptly to prevent damage.
3. **Fall**:
   - **Prepare for Winter**: Winterize your home by insulating pipes, checking weatherstripping on doors and windows, and preparing your heating system.
   - **Clean Gutters**: Clean gutters and downspouts to prepare for winter weather. Remove leaves and debris to prevent ice dams and water damage.
4. **Winter**:
   - **Inspect Insulation**: Check insulation in attics, basements, and crawl spaces to ensure that your home is adequately protected from the cold.
   - **Monitor for Ice Dams**: Inspect your roof and gutters for ice dams, which can cause water to back up and leak into your home. Address any issues to prevent water damage.

Managing Repairs and Upgrades

1. **Prioritizing Repairs**:
   - **Assess Urgency**: Prioritize repairs based on their urgency and potential impact on your home. Address safety issues and structural concerns first, followed by cosmetic or minor repairs.
   - **Obtain Multiple Quotes**: For significant repairs or upgrades, obtain quotes from multiple contractors to ensure competitive pricing and quality workmanship.
2. **Hiring Professionals**:
   - **Research and Vet Contractors**: Research and vet contractors to find qualified professionals for repairs or renovations. Check references, reviews, and credentials to ensure that you're hiring reputable individuals.
   - **Check Licenses and Insurance**: Ensure that contractors are licensed and insured to protect yourself from potential liabilities and ensure that work is performed to code.
3. **Planning Home Improvements**:
   - **Set a Budget**: Plan and budget for home improvements or upgrades. Consider the cost of materials, labor, and any potential additional expenses.
   - **Consult with Professionals**: For major projects, consult with architects, designers, or contractors to develop a plan that meets your needs and enhances your home's value.

"The Art of Negotiation: Home Buying Edition"

Maintaining Home Value

1. **Regular Cleaning**:
   - **Deep Clean**: Perform deep cleaning of your home regularly to maintain a fresh and healthy living environment. This includes cleaning carpets, upholstery, and hard-to-reach areas.
   - **Address Stains and Damage**: Promptly address any stains, damage, or wear on surfaces to prevent long-term issues and maintain the appearance of your home.
2. **Updating and Renovating**:
   - **Refresh Aesthetics**: Consider updating paint, flooring, or fixtures to refresh the appearance of your home. Small updates can have a significant impact on your home's overall look and value.
   - **Plan for Major Renovations**: Plan and budget for major renovations or upgrades that can enhance the functionality and value of your home. Research trends and consult with professionals to ensure that improvements align with your goals.

Conclusion

Maintaining your home is an ongoing process that involves regular inspections, seasonal upkeep, and managing repairs and upgrades. By following a structured maintenance plan, addressing issues promptly, and investing in home improvements, you can keep your home in excellent condition, preserve its value, and enjoy a comfortable and functional living environment. Effective home maintenance not only protects your investment but also enhances your overall quality of life.

Chapter 11: Energy Efficiency and Sustainability: Reducing Costs and Environmental Impact

Introduction to Energy Efficiency and Sustainability

Energy efficiency and sustainability are important considerations for modern homeowners. By adopting energy-efficient practices and making sustainable choices, you can reduce your utility bills, lower your environmental impact, and enhance the comfort of your home. This chapter explores strategies for improving energy efficiency, incorporating sustainable practices, and making eco-friendly upgrades to your home.

Improving Energy Efficiency

1. **Insulation and Weatherproofing**:
   - **Upgrade Insulation**: Proper insulation helps keep your home comfortable by reducing heat loss in winter and keeping it cool in summer. Consider upgrading insulation in your attic, walls, and floors to improve energy efficiency.
   - **Seal Leaks and Gaps**: Check for and seal any gaps or leaks around windows, doors, and other openings. Use weatherstripping, caulk, or foam to prevent drafts and improve your home's energy efficiency.

"The Art of Negotiation: Home Buying Edition"

2. **Energy-Efficient Windows and Doors**:
   o **Install Energy-Efficient Windows**: Energy-efficient windows reduce heat transfer and improve insulation. Look for windows with low-E coatings and double or triple glazing to enhance performance.
   o **Upgrade Doors**: Replace old or inefficient doors with energy-efficient models. Insulated doors and weatherstripping can help prevent heat loss and improve your home's energy efficiency.
3. **Efficient Heating and Cooling Systems**:
   o **Upgrade HVAC Systems**: Invest in an energy-efficient heating, ventilation, and air conditioning (HVAC) system. Look for systems with high Seasonal Energy Efficiency Ratio (SEER) ratings and ENERGY STAR® certification.
   o **Install Programmable Thermostats**: Programmable thermostats allow you to set heating and cooling schedules based on your daily routine. This can reduce energy consumption and lower your utility bills.
4. **Lighting and Appliances**:
   o **Switch to LED Lighting**: LED bulbs are more energy-efficient and longer-lasting than traditional incandescent bulbs. Replace outdated bulbs with LEDs to reduce energy use and improve lighting quality.
   o **Choose Energy-Efficient Appliances**: When replacing appliances, select models with ENERGY STAR® certification. These appliances use less energy and water, leading to lower utility bills and a smaller environmental footprint.

Incorporating Sustainable Practices

1. **Water Conservation**:
   o **Install Low-Flow Fixtures**: Replace standard faucets, showerheads, and toilets with low-flow models to reduce water consumption without sacrificing performance.
   o **Use Water-Efficient Landscaping**: Implement water-saving practices in your garden, such as using drought-resistant plants, installing drip irrigation systems, and collecting rainwater for watering plants.
2. **Renewable Energy Sources**:
   o **Solar Power**: Consider installing solar panels on your roof to generate renewable energy and reduce your reliance on grid electricity. Solar power can lower your utility bills and provide a sustainable energy source for your home.
   o **Solar Water Heaters**: Solar water heaters use sunlight to heat water for your home, reducing the need for conventional water heating methods and lowering energy consumption.
3. **Sustainable Materials**:
   o **Use Eco-Friendly Building Materials**: When making renovations or building new structures, choose sustainable materials such as bamboo, reclaimed wood, or recycled metal. These materials have a lower environmental impact and contribute to a greener home.
   o **Recycling and Reuse**: Incorporate recycling and reuse practices in your home renovation projects. Salvage materials, repurpose items, and recycle waste to minimize environmental impact.

"The Art of Negotiation: Home Buying Edition"

Making Eco-Friendly Upgrades

1. **Green Roofing**:
   - **Install Green Roofs**: Green roofs, also known as living roofs, involve growing vegetation on your roof to improve insulation, reduce stormwater runoff, and enhance the aesthetic appeal of your home.
   - **Cool Roofs**: Cool roofs reflect more sunlight and absorb less heat than traditional roofs. Consider upgrading to a cool roof to reduce cooling costs and improve energy efficiency.
2. **Home Automation**:
   - **Smart Home Technology**: Implement smart home devices to monitor and control energy use more effectively. Smart thermostats, lighting systems, and appliances can be programmed or controlled remotely to optimize energy consumption.
   - **Energy Monitoring Systems**: Use energy monitoring systems to track and analyze your home's energy use. These systems can help identify areas for improvement and provide insights into how to reduce consumption.
3. **Eco-Friendly Landscaping**:
   - **Plant Trees and Shrubs**: Trees and shrubs provide shade, reduce heat absorption, and improve air quality. Planting strategically around your home can help reduce cooling costs and enhance overall comfort.
   - **Native Plants**: Choose native plants for your landscaping, as they are adapted to local conditions and require less water and maintenance.

Financial Incentives and Rebates

1. **Tax Credits and Incentives**:
   - **Federal and State Programs**: Research available tax credits and incentives for energy-efficient upgrades and renewable energy installations. Federal, state, and local programs may offer financial benefits for making eco-friendly improvements.
   - **Utility Rebates**: Many utility companies offer rebates for energy-efficient appliances and home upgrades. Check with your local utility provider to see what programs are available.
2. **Financing Options**:
   - **Energy-Efficient Mortgages**: Some mortgage programs offer financing options for energy-efficient home improvements. Explore these options to finance upgrades and save on long-term energy costs.
   - **Green Loans**: Green loans are specifically designed for financing eco-friendly upgrades. Look into these loan options to fund your sustainable home projects.

Conclusion

Adopting energy-efficient practices and making sustainable upgrades can significantly impact your home's energy consumption, utility costs, and environmental footprint. By implementing strategies such as improving insulation, using energy-efficient appliances, and incorporating renewable energy sources, you can create a more comfortable, cost-effective, and eco-friendly living environment. Staying informed about available incentives and rebates can also help you make financially savvy decisions while contributing to a greener future.

Chapter 12: Understanding Property Taxes and Insurance: Managing Costs and Coverage

Introduction to Property Taxes and Insurance

Property taxes and insurance are significant financial aspects of homeownership that can impact your overall budget and financial planning. Understanding how property taxes are assessed and how to choose the right insurance coverage is crucial for managing these costs effectively. This chapter provides a detailed overview of property taxes, home insurance, and strategies for managing both.

Understanding Property Taxes

1. **How Property Taxes Are Assessed**:
   - **Property Valuation**: Property taxes are based on the assessed value of your home, which is determined by your local tax assessor. This valuation takes into account the property's market value, improvements, and other factors.
   - **Tax Rate**: The property tax rate, also known as the mill rate, is set by local government authorities. It is expressed as a percentage of the assessed value and can vary depending on your location and the services provided by your municipality.
2. **Appealing Your Property Assessment**:
   - **Review Your Assessment**: Regularly review your property's assessed value to ensure it is accurate. Compare it with recent sales of similar properties in your area to assess its fairness.
   - **Appeal Process**: If you believe your property's assessed value is too high, you can appeal the assessment. The appeal process typically involves filing a formal request with your local tax assessor's office and providing evidence to support your claim.
3. **Managing Property Tax Payments**:
   - **Payment Options**: Property taxes are usually paid annually or semi-annually. Check with your local tax authority to understand your payment options and deadlines.
   - **Budgeting for Taxes**: Set aside funds for property tax payments in advance. Consider creating a dedicated savings account to manage this expense and avoid financial strain when payments are due.
4. **Tax Deductions and Exemptions**:
   - **Homestead Exemptions**: Some states offer homestead exemptions that reduce the taxable value of your primary residence. Check if you qualify for any exemptions and apply for them as needed.

"The Art of Negotiation: Home Buying Edition"

- **Property Tax Deductions**: Property taxes are generally deductible on your federal income tax return. Keep records of your property tax payments and consult with a tax professional to ensure you maximize your deductions.

Understanding Home Insurance

1. **Types of Home Insurance Coverage**:
    - **Dwelling Coverage**: This covers the cost of repairing or rebuilding your home if it is damaged or destroyed by covered perils such as fire, storm, or vandalism.
    - **Personal Property Coverage**: This covers the cost of replacing personal belongings such as furniture, clothing, and electronics if they are damaged or stolen.
    - **Liability Coverage**: This provides protection if someone is injured on your property or if you are responsible for damage to someone else's property. It helps cover legal expenses and potential settlements.
    - **Additional Living Expenses (ALE)**: ALE coverage helps pay for temporary housing and living expenses if you are unable to live in your home due to a covered loss.
2. **Choosing the Right Insurance Policy**:
    - **Evaluate Your Needs**: Assess your home's value, personal belongings, and potential risks to determine the appropriate level of coverage. Consider factors such as location, property value, and local risks (e.g., flooding or earthquakes).
    - **Compare Policies**: Obtain quotes from multiple insurance providers and compare coverage options, deductibles, and premiums. Look for policies that offer comprehensive protection at a competitive rate.
3. **Managing Insurance Costs**:
    - **Increase Deductibles**: Choosing a higher deductible can lower your insurance premium. Ensure that you have sufficient savings to cover the deductible if you need to file a claim.
    - **Bundle Policies**: Many insurance providers offer discounts if you bundle home insurance with other policies, such as auto insurance. Explore bundling options to save on premiums.
4. **Regularly Reviewing and Updating Coverage**:
    - **Review Annually**: Review your insurance policy annually to ensure it still meets your needs. Update coverage limits and personal property values as needed to reflect changes in your home and belongings.
    - **Report Changes**: Inform your insurance provider of any significant changes to your property, such as renovations or new valuables. This ensures that your policy remains accurate and provides adequate coverage.

Preparing for Insurance Claims

1. **Documenting Your Property**:
    - **Create an Inventory**: Maintain an up-to-date inventory of your personal belongings, including photographs or videos. This documentation can be useful

when filing a claim and helps ensure you are adequately compensated for lost or damaged items.
    - **Keep Records**: Keep records of home improvements, repairs, and maintenance. These documents can support your claim and demonstrate the condition and value of your property.
2. **Filing a Claim**:
    - **Report Damage Promptly**: Contact your insurance provider as soon as you discover damage or loss. Provide detailed information and documentation to support your claim.
    - **Work with Adjusters**: Insurance adjusters will assess the damage and determine the amount of compensation. Cooperate with them and provide any additional information they may require.
3. **Resolving Disputes**:
    - **Review Policy Terms**: If you disagree with the insurance company's settlement offer, review your policy terms and coverage details. Understand your rights and the terms of your policy.
    - **Seek Mediation**: If necessary, seek mediation or arbitration to resolve disputes with your insurance provider. This can help ensure a fair resolution and avoid lengthy legal battles.

Conclusion

Managing property taxes and home insurance is a crucial aspect of homeownership that requires careful planning and attention. By understanding how property taxes are assessed, appealing unfair assessments, and budgeting for tax payments, you can effectively manage this financial obligation. Choosing the right insurance policy and maintaining adequate coverage protects your home and belongings while providing peace of mind. Regularly reviewing your insurance and preparing for potential claims ensures that you are well-prepared for any challenges that may arise. With a proactive approach, you can effectively manage these costs and safeguard your investment in your home.

Chapter 13: Home Renovations and Upgrades: Enhancing Value and Functionality

Introduction to Home Renovations and Upgrades

Home renovations and upgrades are not only about improving aesthetics but also about enhancing the functionality and value of your property. Whether you are planning to remodel your kitchen, add a bathroom, or update your home's exterior, understanding the process and making informed decisions can lead to successful and satisfying outcomes. This chapter provides a comprehensive guide to planning, executing, and managing home renovations and upgrades, with tips for maximizing your investment and minimizing stress.

Planning Your Renovation

"The Art of Negotiation: Home Buying Edition"

1. **Define Your Goals**:
   - **Identify Objectives**: Determine what you want to achieve with your renovation. Whether it's increasing space, improving functionality, or enhancing curb appeal, having clear objectives will guide your decision-making process.
   - **Set a Budget**: Establish a realistic budget for your renovation project. Include costs for materials, labor, permits, and any unexpected expenses. Allocate funds for both the essential and optional aspects of the project.
2. **Research and Design**:
   - **Gather Inspiration**: Collect ideas and inspiration from magazines, websites, and home improvement shows. Create a mood board or design plan to visualize your desired outcome.
   - **Consult with Professionals**: Consider hiring an architect, designer, or contractor to help refine your ideas and develop a detailed design plan. Professionals can provide valuable insights and ensure that your renovation meets your needs and adheres to building codes.
3. **Obtain Permits and Approvals**:
   - **Check Local Regulations**: Determine if your renovation requires permits or approvals from local authorities. Common projects that may need permits include structural changes, electrical work, and plumbing modifications.
   - **Submit Applications**: Apply for necessary permits and approvals before starting the renovation. Ensure that all required documentation is submitted and approved to avoid delays or legal issues.

Executing the Renovation

1. **Hiring Contractors and Tradespeople**:
   - **Select Qualified Professionals**: Choose reputable contractors and tradespeople for your renovation project. Obtain references, check reviews, and verify licenses and insurance.
   - **Get Multiple Quotes**: Request quotes from several contractors to compare pricing and services. Ensure that quotes are detailed and include all aspects of the project.
2. **Managing the Construction Process**:
   - **Establish a Timeline**: Work with your contractor to develop a realistic timeline for the renovation. Factor in time for each phase of the project, including demolition, construction, and finishing.
   - **Monitor Progress**: Regularly check on the progress of the renovation to ensure that it is proceeding according to plan. Address any issues or concerns with your contractor promptly.
3. **Handling Unexpected Issues**:
   - **Prepare for Contingencies**: Be prepared for potential challenges or unexpected issues during the renovation. These may include structural problems, delays in materials, or unforeseen costs.
   - **Communicate with Your Contractor**: Maintain open communication with your contractor throughout the project. Discuss any changes or issues that arise and work together to find solutions.

"The Art of Negotiation: Home Buying Edition"

Upgrading Specific Areas

1. **Kitchen Renovations**:
   - **Enhance Functionality**: Focus on improving the functionality of your kitchen by updating appliances, adding storage solutions, and optimizing the layout. Consider incorporating energy-efficient appliances and modern fixtures.
   - **Update Aesthetics**: Refresh the appearance of your kitchen with new countertops, cabinets, and flooring. Choose materials and finishes that complement your home's style and enhance its overall appeal.
2. **Bathroom Upgrades**:
   - **Improve Comfort**: Upgrade your bathroom to enhance comfort and convenience. Consider installing a new shower or tub, adding heated floors, or updating fixtures for a more luxurious experience.
   - **Optimize Space**: If space is limited, explore options for optimizing your bathroom layout. This may include installing space-saving storage solutions or redesigning the layout to improve functionality.
3. **Exterior Enhancements**:
   - **Boost Curb Appeal**: Improve your home's curb appeal with exterior upgrades such as new siding, roofing, landscaping, and outdoor lighting. These enhancements can significantly impact the overall appearance and value of your property.
   - **Energy Efficiency**: Consider energy-efficient upgrades for the exterior of your home, such as installing new windows or doors, adding insulation, or upgrading to a more efficient HVAC system.

Maximizing Return on Investment

1. **Focus on High-Impact Upgrades**:
   - **Prioritize Projects**: Invest in renovations that offer the highest return on investment (ROI). Kitchen and bathroom remodels, energy-efficient upgrades, and curb appeal enhancements often yield significant value increases.
   - **Quality Materials**: Use high-quality materials and workmanship to ensure that your upgrades are durable and add long-term value to your home.
2. **Consider Market Trends**:
   - **Research Trends**: Stay informed about current market trends and buyer preferences. Renovations that align with popular trends or address common buyer needs can enhance the appeal and value of your property.
   - **Consult Real Estate Experts**: Seek advice from real estate professionals to understand which upgrades are most likely to attract buyers and provide a good return on investment.

Managing Costs and Expectations

1. **Stay Within Budget**:

"The Art of Negotiation: Home Buying Edition"

- o **Track Expenses**: Keep a detailed record of all renovation expenses to ensure that you stay within budget. Monitor spending and make adjustments as needed to avoid overspending.
- o **Plan for Contingencies**: Set aside a contingency fund for unexpected expenses. Having a financial buffer can help you manage unforeseen costs without disrupting the renovation.

2. **Set Realistic Expectations**:
    - o **Understand Limitations**: Recognize the limitations of your renovation project and manage your expectations accordingly. Some changes may require additional time, effort, or expense.
    - o **Be Patient**: Renovations can be disruptive and may take longer than anticipated. Maintain patience and flexibility throughout the process to achieve the best results.

Conclusion

Home renovations and upgrades offer an opportunity to enhance the functionality, aesthetics, and value of your property. By carefully planning your project, selecting qualified professionals, and managing costs effectively, you can achieve successful and satisfying results. Focus on high-impact upgrades, stay informed about market trends, and maintain realistic expectations to maximize the return on your investment. With thoughtful planning and execution, you can create a home that meets your needs and adds long-term value to your property.

Chapter 14: Navigating the Real Estate Market: Buying and Selling Strategies

Introduction to the Real Estate Market

Navigating the real estate market can be a complex and challenging process, whether you are buying or selling a home. Understanding market dynamics, employing effective strategies, and being prepared for the various stages of the transaction can lead to successful outcomes. This chapter explores essential strategies for both buying and selling homes, providing insights into market trends, negotiation tactics, and tips for making informed decisions.

Buying a Home

1. **Understanding Market Conditions**:
    - o **Market Trends**: Stay informed about current real estate market trends, including supply and demand, interest rates, and local housing prices. Understanding these trends can help you make strategic decisions and identify the best time to buy.
    - o **Local Market Insights**: Research the local housing market in your desired area. Analyze recent sales data, neighborhood trends, and property values to gauge the market and find suitable options.
2. **Financing Your Purchase**:

"The Art of Negotiation: Home Buying Edition"

- o **Mortgage Pre-Approval**: Obtain mortgage pre-approval to determine your budget and strengthen your position as a buyer. Pre-approval provides a clear idea of your borrowing capacity and shows sellers that you are a serious buyer.
- o **Explore Loan Options**: Compare different mortgage loan options, including fixed-rate and adjustable-rate mortgages. Consider factors such as interest rates, loan terms, and down payment requirements to find the best fit for your financial situation.

3. **House Hunting**:
   - o **Create a Wish List**: Define your criteria for a new home, including location, size, features, and amenities. Prioritize your must-have items and preferences to guide your search.
   - o **Work with a Real Estate Agent**: Partner with a qualified real estate agent who knows the local market and can help you find properties that meet your criteria. An experienced agent can provide valuable insights, negotiate on your behalf, and assist with the buying process.
4. **Making an Offer**:
   - o **Evaluate the Property**: Assess the property's condition, value, and potential issues before making an offer. Consider conducting a home inspection to uncover any hidden problems.
   - o **Negotiate Terms**: Work with your agent to develop a competitive offer based on market conditions and comparable sales. Be prepared to negotiate terms, including price, contingencies, and closing dates.
5. **Closing the Deal**:
   - o **Review Closing Documents**: Carefully review all closing documents, including the purchase agreement, loan documents, and settlement statement. Ensure that all terms are accurate and reflect the agreed-upon conditions.
   - o **Complete the Transaction**: Finalize the purchase by signing the necessary documents, making the required payments, and transferring ownership. Celebrate your new home and begin the process of moving in and settling down.

Selling a Home

1. **Preparing Your Home for Sale**:
   - o **Enhance Curb Appeal**: Improve the exterior appearance of your home to attract potential buyers. Consider landscaping, painting, and minor repairs to make a positive first impression.
   - o **Staging Your Home**: Stage your home to highlight its best features and create a welcoming atmosphere. Arrange furniture, declutter, and make necessary repairs to showcase the property in its best light.
2. **Setting the Right Price**:
   - o **Conduct a Comparative Market Analysis (CMA)**: Work with your real estate agent to perform a CMA, which analyzes recent sales of similar properties in your area. This analysis helps determine a competitive and realistic listing price.
   - o **Consider Market Conditions**: Factor in current market conditions, including supply and demand, interest rates, and local trends, when setting your price. Adjust your pricing strategy as needed to remain competitive.

"The Art of Negotiation: Home Buying Edition"

3. **Marketing Your Property**:
   - **Online Listings and Advertising**: Utilize online platforms, social media, and real estate websites to market your property. High-quality photos, detailed descriptions, and virtual tours can attract more potential buyers.
   - **Host Open Houses**: Schedule open houses to allow prospective buyers to view your property in person. Provide information about the home and neighborhood to generate interest and encourage offers.
4. **Negotiating Offers**:
   - **Review Offers Carefully**: Evaluate each offer based on price, contingencies, and buyer qualifications. Consider the strength of the buyer's financial position and their readiness to close the deal.
   - **Negotiate Terms**: Negotiate terms with potential buyers to reach a mutually agreeable contract. Be open to counteroffers and work with your agent to address any concerns or requests from buyers.
5. **Closing the Sale**:
   - **Review Closing Documents**: Thoroughly review all closing documents, including the sales agreement, settlement statement, and any required disclosures. Ensure that all terms and conditions are correct.
   - **Complete the Transaction**: Finalize the sale by signing the necessary documents, transferring ownership, and receiving payment. Prepare for the transition and plan for your next move.

Navigating Market Challenges

1. **Dealing with Market Fluctuations**:
   - **Adapt to Changes**: Be prepared to adapt to market fluctuations and changing conditions. Stay informed about economic factors, interest rate changes, and local market trends that may impact your transaction.
   - **Seek Professional Advice**: Consult with real estate professionals, such as agents and financial advisors, to navigate challenges and make informed decisions during periods of market uncertainty.
2. **Managing Emotional Factors**:
   - **Stay Objective**: Buying or selling a home can be an emotional experience. Focus on your goals and needs rather than personal attachments or sentimental value. Maintain a clear perspective to make rational decisions.
   - **Communicate Effectively**: Communicate openly and effectively with your real estate agent, buyers, or sellers to address concerns and resolve issues. Clear communication helps facilitate a smoother transaction process.

Conclusion

Navigating the real estate market requires careful planning, informed decision-making, and effective strategies. Whether you are buying or selling a home, understanding market conditions, preparing your property, and managing negotiations can lead to successful outcomes. By working with qualified professionals and staying informed about market trends, you can make well-informed decisions and achieve your real estate goals. With a strategic approach and a clear understanding of the process, you can successfully navigate the complexities of buying and selling a home.

Chapter 15: Preparing for Moving Day: Tips and Best Practices

Introduction to Moving Day

Moving day is a significant milestone in the home buying or selling process. Proper preparation and organization can make the transition smoother, reduce stress, and ensure that everything is handled efficiently. This chapter offers practical tips and best practices for preparing for moving day, including packing strategies, logistics, and ensuring a seamless transition to your new home.

Planning and Organizing

1. **Create a Moving Checklist**:
   - **Develop a Timeline**: Start by creating a moving checklist with tasks to complete before, during, and after the move. Include key dates, such as when to start packing, when to notify utilities, and the moving day itself.
   - **Assign Responsibilities**: If you're moving with others, assign specific tasks to family members or roommates. This could include packing particular rooms, organizing supplies, or coordinating with the moving company.
2. **Hire Professional Movers**:
   - **Research Moving Companies**: Research and compare moving companies to find one that fits your needs. Check reviews, ask for recommendations, and ensure that the movers are licensed and insured.
   - **Get Quotes**: Obtain quotes from multiple moving companies and compare services, prices, and insurance options. Make sure to get a written estimate and clarify any additional fees.
3. **Notify Relevant Parties**:
   - **Update Address**: Notify relevant parties of your change of address, including the postal service, banks, insurance companies, and subscription services. Update your address with these organizations to ensure that you continue to receive important mail and services.
   - **Inform Utilities**: Contact utility companies to schedule disconnection at your old home and connection at your new home. Arrange for services such as electricity, water, gas, internet, and cable to be set up before your move-in date.

Packing and Preparation

1. **Sort and Declutter**:
   - **Purge Unnecessary Items**: Before you start packing, sort through your belongings and declutter. Donate, sell, or discard items that you no longer need or use. This will reduce the amount of stuff you need to move and make the process more efficient.

- **"The Art of Negotiation: Home Buying Edition"**

    - o **Organize by Category**: Group similar items together, such as books, kitchenware, and clothing. This will make packing and unpacking easier and help you keep track of your belongings.
  2. **Pack Efficiently**:
     - o **Use Quality Packing Materials**: Invest in sturdy moving boxes, packing tape, bubble wrap, and packing paper. Proper packing materials protect your items and prevent damage during the move.
     - o **Label Boxes**: Clearly label each box with its contents and the room it belongs to. Use color-coded labels or markers to make identification easier and streamline the unpacking process.
     - o **Pack Essentials Separately**: Pack a separate box with essential items you'll need immediately upon arrival at your new home. This could include toiletries, a change of clothes, basic kitchen items, and important documents.
  3. **Prepare for Moving Day**:
     - o **Create a Moving Day Kit**: Prepare a moving day kit with essentials such as snacks, drinks, a first aid kit, tools, and any important documents. Having these items readily available will help you stay organized and comfortable throughout the day.
     - o **Protect Your Home**: Protect your old and new homes during the move by covering floors and walls. Use moving blankets or plastic sheeting to prevent scratches and dents.

Managing the Move

1. **Coordinate with Movers**:
   - o **Confirm Details**: Confirm the details with your moving company, including the time of arrival, the number of movers, and any special instructions. Ensure that they have all necessary information about your move.
   - o **Supervise the Move**: Be present on moving day to supervise the process and address any issues that arise. Provide clear instructions to the movers and ensure that they handle your belongings with care.
2. **Check Inventory**:
   - o **Conduct a Walk-Through**: Before the movers leave, conduct a walk-through of your old home to ensure that nothing is left behind. Check all rooms, closets, and storage areas to confirm that everything has been packed.
   - o **Inspect Items**: As your belongings are unloaded at your new home, inspect them for any damage. Report any issues to the moving company promptly to address them.

Settling Into Your New Home

1. **Unpack Strategically**:
   - o **Prioritize Rooms**: Unpack essential rooms first, such as the kitchen and bedrooms. Set up necessary items and ensure that you have everything you need for daily living.

- **Organize as You Go**: As you unpack, take the time to organize your belongings and arrange them in a way that suits your new space. This will help you settle in more quickly and create a functional living environment.
2. **Explore Your New Neighborhood**:
    - **Get Acquainted**: Take some time to explore your new neighborhood and familiarize yourself with local amenities. Visit nearby stores, restaurants, parks, and community centers to get to know your new surroundings.
    - **Introduce Yourself**: Meet your new neighbors and introduce yourself. Building relationships with those around you can help you feel more at home and integrate into the community.
3. **Update Records and Information**:
    - **Register Your Vehicle**: If you've moved to a new area, update your vehicle registration and driver's license with your new address. Check local regulations for any additional requirements.
    - **Transfer School Records**: If you have children, transfer their school records to their new school. Contact the school administration to ensure a smooth transition for your children.

Conclusion

Preparing for moving day involves careful planning, organization, and coordination to ensure a smooth transition to your new home. By creating a comprehensive moving checklist, hiring reliable movers, and packing efficiently, you can minimize stress and make the process more manageable. Once you arrive at your new home, unpack strategically, explore your new neighborhood, and update your records to settle in quickly and comfortably. With thoughtful preparation and execution, you can successfully navigate the moving process and begin enjoying your new living space.

It looks like we've covered all 15 chapters for your book, "The Art of Negotiation: Home Buying Edition." Here's a quick summary of the content we've created:

1. **Introduction to Home Buying and Negotiation**: Overview of the home buying process and the importance of negotiation.
2. **Setting Your Budget and Financing Options**: How to determine your budget and explore various financing options.
3. **Finding the Right Real Estate Agent**: Tips for selecting an effective real estate agent and building a strong working relationship.
4. **Researching and Choosing a Neighborhood**: Strategies for evaluating neighborhoods and finding the right location for your home.
5. **Understanding Market Conditions and Trends**: Insight into real estate market dynamics and how to use them to your advantage.
6. **Evaluating and Making an Offer on a Home**: How to assess a property and make a competitive offer.
7. **Negotiating the Purchase Agreement**: Key strategies for negotiating terms and conditions of the purchase agreement.

"The Art of Negotiation: Home Buying Edition"

8. **Conducting Home Inspections and Assessments**: Importance of home inspections and how to address any issues that arise.
9. **Navigating the Closing Process**: Detailed steps involved in closing the deal and finalizing the purchase.
10. **Post-Purchase Considerations**: What to do after purchasing your home, including moving in and settling down.
11. **Legal and Regulatory Aspects of Home Buying**: Understanding legal requirements and regulatory aspects related to home buying.
12. **Understanding Property Taxes and Insurance**: Managing property taxes and choosing the right insurance coverage.
13. **Home Renovations and Upgrades**: Planning and executing renovations and upgrades to enhance value and functionality.
14. **Navigating the Real Estate Market: Buying and Selling Strategies**: Strategies for both buying and selling homes effectively.
15. **Preparing for Moving Day: Tips and Best Practices**: Practical advice for a smooth and efficient moving process.

www.ingramcontent.com/pod-product-compliance
Lightning Source LLC
Chambersburg PA
CBHW080435240526

45479CB00016B/1308